GET MOVING IN THE CITY

WRITTEN BY
JACKIE HERON

ILLUSTRATED BY
TATEVIK AVAKYAN

magic wagon

Content Consultant:
Jonathan Martin
Physical Education Teacher, Nova Classical Academy

VISIT US AT WWW.ABDOPUBLISHING.COM

Published by Magic Wagon, a division of the ABDO Group, PO Box 398166, Minneapolis, MN 55439. Copyright © 2012 by Abdo Consulting Group, Inc. International copyrights reserved in all countries. All rights reserved. No part of this book may be reproduced in any form without written permission from the publisher.

Looking Glass Library™ is a trademark and logo of Magic Wagon.

Printed in the United States of America, North Mankato, Minnesota.
102011
012012

 THIS BOOK CONTAINS AT LEAST 10% RECYCLED MATERIALS.

Text by Jackie Heron
Illustrations by Tatevik Avakyan
Edited by Melissa York
Design and production by Emily Love

Library of Congress Cataloging-in-Publication Data

Heron, Jackie.
  Get moving in the city / by Jackie Heron ; illustrated by Tatevik Avakyan.
      p. cm. — (Move and get healthy!)
  Includes index.
  ISBN 978-1-61641-859-5
  1. Physical fitness for children—Juvenile literature. I. Avakyan, Tatevik, 1983- ill. II. Title.
  GV443.H43 2012
  613.7083—dc23
                            2011033081

TABLE OF CONTENTS

PLAYING IN THE CITY

There are many places you can play in the city! Ask a grown-up where you can play outside. Play inside at your school or community center. You can even get moving at home in your own room!

STAY SAFE

Playing in the street is not safe. Don't play near construction sites. Playing near water? You need a grown-up nearby.

5

HAPPY MUSCLES

Eat right, move right, and feel right. Your muscles are happy when you eat healthy foods. You become fitter and stronger.

Muscles like to move, too. Move your muscles every day. Then your body will work for you. You won't hurt or get too tired. That's when you'll feel your best.

7

YOUR BODY TEAM

Your body is a group of teams. The teams all work together. Your digestive system breaks down food and turns it into energy. Your muscular-skeletal system is your muscles and bones. It uses that energy to move.

You are the team captain. You decide what to eat and when and how to move.

SAFETY FIRST

Here are some tips to keep you comfortable and safe when you exercise.

✳ Listen to grown-ups! They will tell you where it's safe to play.

✳ Don't play outside alone.

✳ Wear sunscreen. It protects your skin from the sun.

✳ Need to cross the street? What if you meet a stranger or a stray dog? Make a plan with a grown-up. Know what to do if something unsafe happens.

Dress for the weather and wear gym shoes.

Drink lots of water and eat healthy foods. This gives you energy to play longer.

Follow the rules at a park, playground, or event.

12

SMART MOVES

Your body makes endorphins when you exercise. Endorphins make you feel less pain. They also make you happy! Endorphins help you sleep better, learn faster, and look and feel healthier.

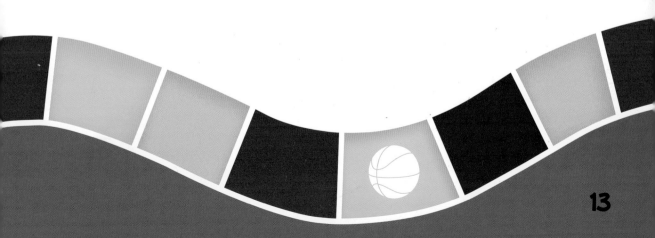

KEEP TRACK

Pick a hard activity you like and do it for 10 minutes. Do an easier one you like for 20 minutes. Find a sheet of paper. Write the date, activity, and time you spent exercising.

Track what you do every day. The activities will get easier each time. You can change your routine, too. What new activity will you try?

WHY KEEP TRACK?

There are many good reasons to track your exercise. You will see when you get better. You make fitness goals and know when you meet them. You will feel good about yourself, too.

15

WEIGH IN

There's good weight and bad weight. Your body has muscle tissue and fatty tissue. A piece of muscle tissue weighs more than a piece of fatty tissue the same size.

Are your muscles fit and toned? Check out your muscles in the mirror. Look at your face, tummy, waist, arms, and legs. Smile. Show your biceps!

GET ACTIVE!

Think of ways to work your upper body. You could:

- Help a neighbor with yard work or work in a community garden.
- Go to the park. Hang on the monkey bars or push someone on the swings.
- Learn to play tennis at your community center.

Next, work your lower body:

❊ Skip down the block. Raise your knees as high as you can. Can you touch your chest?

❊ Run relay races with a team.

❊ Go biking on a bike path or go roller-skating at a rink.

Feel your muscles and bones getting stronger!

Fat

Muscle

WHAT IS MUSCLE TISSUE?

Muscle tissue is firm. It has small ridges like string that has been scrunched together tightly. Fatty tissue is soft and mushy.

When you are active you will find your best weight. You may lose fat but still weigh the same. This is because you have more muscle. Your muscles will be stronger and stretch easier.

MUSCLE AND FAT

One pound of muscle is about the size of an orange. One pound of fat is about three times as large.

21

A MOMENT FOR MUSCLES

You can move your muscles anytime and anywhere. Stand up and stretch for the ceiling. Bend at your waist and let your arms dangle. Stand up straight again. Rise up on your toes a few times.

Now run in place as fast as you can and count to 100. Stand straight and make big circles with your arms. Are you sweating yet? Run in place and move your arms together this time.

YOUR BODY TYPE

The more you move your muscles, the more you will see a change in your body. Too much fat can cause illnesses. But being underweight isn't healthy either.

Don't compare yourself to others. Your best weight depends on your height, age, and body type. Be comfortable and positive about your body. Look your own best!

CALCULATE YOUR BMI

A doctor can find your Body Mass Index, or BMI. BMI measures how much muscle and fat a person has. You can find your BMI yourself! Ask a grown-up for help. Measure your weight and height. There are tools online to find your BMI. Make sure you use a tool for children. Put your height and weight into the online tool. It will tell your BMI and what it means.

HAVE FUN!

Here are more activities you can do in the city!

GROOVY SIDEWALK

Use sidewalk chalk to draw your own obstacle course. Here's one example: Put on your helmet and ride a scooter on the wavy line. Hop on each circle. Do ten jumping jacks inside the triangle. Run to the dotted line. Use a stopwatch or make one friend the counter. Who was the fastest?

HOW HIGH? HOW FAR?

Can you spin a ball on one finger? Count how many seconds before it falls off. Throw the ball up and clap your hands. How many times did you clap? See how many times you and a friend can toss the ball without dropping it.

YOUR TURN!

Try making up your own game. First, find five things. Make sure they do not have sharp points. Run your choices by a grown-up. Items might be: a pillow, a balloon, an old phone book, a pair of socks, and a spoon.

How can you use those things to move? Can you dance on the phone book without falling off? Use just your head to keep the balloon off the ground. Keep playing until you're hot and sweaty . . . or cracking up!

How many ways can you think of today to keep moving?

KEEP MOVING

1. When you watch TV, take breaks to do jumping jacks. How many jumping jacks can you do the first time? Can you top your record the next time?

2. Hold a Kid Olympics at your next birthday party. Host the event at a local park for free. Or, rent the gym at a local community center for a couple of hours. Then, decide which events you want to do: three-legged race, balloon toss, obstacle course, foam sword fencing . . . and don't forget the prizes! (A bouquet of dandelions, paper medals, you name it!)

3. Make a mix of your favorite dance music on a CD or your MP3 player. Invite a friend over for a private dance party. Close the door and sing and dance as loudly as you want.

4. Chances are, you can download recorded books from your local library onto an MP3 player. Listen to your favorite books while you walk, run laps, garden, or do chores. It's amazing how long you'll be able to exercise when you're listening to a good story.

5. Volunteer in your community. Work on a community garden. Take a walk with a senior from a senior center. Care for the dogs and cats at an animal shelter. Join a charity run/walk. You'll keep fit and help others at the same time!

WORDS TO KNOW

biceps—the muscles on the inner side of your upper arm.

endorphins—chemicals the body makes that help a person feel better and sleep well.

energy—being able to do things without feeling tired.

muscle—body tissue, or layers of cells, that help the body move.

obstacle course—a path, often a race, made difficult on purpose with things in the way such as water, mud, or items to climb over or under.

routine—a series of things you do the same way every day.

tissue—a group of cells that forms a body part such as an organ or a muscle.

LEARN MORE

BOOKS

Ettinger, Steve. *Wallie Exercises*. New York: Active Spud Press, 2011.

Rockwell, Lizzy. *The Busy Body Book*. New York: Crown, 2011.

Virgilio, Stephen J. *Active Start For Healthy Kids: Activities, Exercises, and Nutritional Tips*. Champaign, IL: Human Kinetics, 2006.

WEB SITES

To learn more about being active in the city, visit ABDO Group online at **www.abdopublishing.com**. Web sites about being active in the city are featured on our Book Links page. These links are routinely monitored and updated to provide the most current information available.

INDEX